Indigo Blues

TONI MACLEAN

authorHOUSE®

AuthorHouse™
1663 Liberty Drive
Bloomington, IN 47403
www.authorhouse.com
Phone: 1 (800) 839-8640

Published by AuthorHouse 11/05/2019

ISBN: 978-1-7283-3477-6 (sc)
ISBN: 978-1-7283-3476-9 (e)

Library of Congress Control Number: 2019918151

Print information available on the last page.

CONTENTS

FOREWORD

I have lived in the West Highlands for 70 years and have seen many changes. When I was a child there was no road to our home and we had to travel by ferry boat or walk over the Bealach the 6 miles to the railhead and the road, and because of the isolation I had no friends but my brother. But we were free as the wind, although we did have to help on the farm, collect and milk the cows, help with the tatties and the hay. When I was 11 I went away to a convent boarding school and then to Dundee University where I studied Social work, but I never got to practice it because I met my husband who wanted to stay at home and fish for shellfish, though I did manage to get some voluntary work in mental health and with delinquent teenagers. By this time there was a road and we were able to build our own house, but still no electricity. We brought up our 4 wonderful boys, and when the youngest one left home I was very lonely and had to find an outlet. I had been writing poetry on and off so with plenty of time to think and ruminate I wrote, and I also took up art which has been my passion ever since ..... any medium including gardening. While the children were small we had the opportunity to live in Greece for a year which was difficult but lovely and got us into travelling ... Europe, Iceland, Cuba, Egypt, Turkey and Australia. A varied and fascinating life and I hope my poems express the depth of that experience Christina Finlay was a young friend who battled mental illness through her art. She contributed some of the illustration to the poems. The others are my own.

NETTLES

I used to ride along this way,
a milk pail on each handlebar,
well balanced, smooth,
when London Pride adorned the wall
where now the nettles grow,
before the road eroded
down to mettling.

They have their uses, nettles.
We used to feed them to the hens,
their odour sharp and pungent
in the steamy mash.
We gathered them when young,
bare-legged, open-handed and unstung.

We're older now, we've grown.
Their stalks are woody, bristling,
leaves toughened, poison-tongued.
And now we keep away,
or wear protective layers
as we try to sidle by,
my childhood friend and I.

NOTHING ADDED

We didn't go to school till I was nine, we played around
the steading, balancing on rafters, up above the cow's warm breath
and sounds oflanguid chewing, shuffiing. We smoked behind the
bales.
On rainy days we lit the bothy stove and battered pancakes with
secreted flour, eggs from the chickens' hidden nests and milk
that the cows let down. They were so used to us, to being
scratched and petted, butted at, they didn't mind.
The mill was derelict but all the cogs still turned, the wheel
a carrousel for riding on, but best of all was when the smithy fire,
goaded by enormous bellows, roared and spat, the glowing metal
sparked, and sweating horses stamped and fretted, waiting to be
shod.
It's all in ruins now, and sold for redevelopment, I went
to school and tried to learn arithmetic, the dates of English kings
in copperplate, and how to play by other peoples rules.

THE FERRY-BOAT

Before the road the boat came twice a week
to bring the mail and messages, and everything
from drums of paraffin and T.V.O. rolled overboard
to float ashore, to visitors in shoes and overcoats
with leather luggage, lowered to the dinghy, still awash
from being towed, and rowed up to the jetty
where they had to jump in case the dinghy
scraped or bumped. Few made it dry.

On stormy days it didn't want to stop, and tried
to sneak along. We had to watch for it,
a slowly growing, rhythmically recurring blur
that tried to hide far out; we'd shout,
and wave a sheet and dance about.
As kids we'd scramble aft
to travel in the wheelhouse where the Whaler
let us steer and gave us cigarettes and beer.
These days I travel more. I drive
from door to door, and shop on line.
And sometimes I go surfing on force nine.

FARQUHAR

I've known him over fifty years, I first
remember him astride a Clydesdale galloping
along the beach, and in the lean-to where
he built his motor-bikes, and made
a waterwheel from rusty cans
tacked to a cycle wheel, to charge their batteries.
A man of gentle words, he saved his breath
for distance running, nearly every year
he won the hill race at the gathering here.
He always led the music on his button-key
as now the piper leads him and his bearers,
old friends taking turns to carry him
this final lap of honour round the field.
I've pushed him in his chair, I've lit
his pipe and doused the fire when he set his bed alight.
And now I follow, with the rest, treading a slow march.

FLASHBACK

The first time that I fell in love, I must have been thirteen,
The marker in my memory--the Everly Brothers' "Dream".
The things that interest gentlemen I then knew nothing of
   With a convent education, and a pop-mag view of love.
The things the others whispered of I tried to get to know
   From the new transistor radio I turned down very low.
   They all seemed so sophisticated, giggling, and free,
   Though the bulk of them were probably as ignorant as me.
And bulky was the word for us [stiletto heels were banned].
   Some amorous adventures in the holidays were planned
   Or boasted of, though very likely most of it was lies,
   Everyone wanted to look good in other people's eyes.
The beehive hairstyles, bobby-socks, smoking behind the gym
   As near as we could get to being grown-up, tall or slim,
   And underneath our desk-lids,where the sisters couldn't see
We stuck hunky coloured posters of Pat Boone,and Bobby Vee.
   I learnt to love a lot of things, like music [not just pop],
   And reading--all the Brontes and Jane Austen on the trot,
   But all the time I was at school romance was on my mind.
   I left as soon as maybe, and left innocence behind.

The sixties were a better time, I'd learnt a bit of cool,
With boys and cars the pace was hot, and breaking late the rule
The mini was in fashion for your wheels and for your bum,
With knee-high boots and skinny tops, and everything was fun.
The race was on, the hunt begun, the perfect man to find,
But nintyfive percent had only one thing on their mind.
The other girls would have their boyfriends staying in the flat,
I wanted a relationship with something more than that.
But there were likely lads among the ones who turned me down,
An Irishman I went to hoolys with in Campden town,
A handsom King's Own Rifleman who taught me how to shoot,
And a very, very amourous Armenian from Beirut.
The wind of change was blowing through our long and tangled
hairs
For flower-power had turned us into hippies wearing flares.
We all had plenty energy for going on the spree
And sitting up all night discussing sociology,
And plenty money, too,for buying music that was new-Rock,
deep, deep soul, and Joni Mitchell's "Blue".
But sometimes I got panicky, as teeth began to lengthen,
And often there were lonely times I'm not prepared to mention
So when I met a hunky guy who wanted me to wife I decided not to
struggle, and gave up the single life.

THE TRIALS

On a sunny day in the middle of May
The motor-bikes begin
To test their skills by climbing hills
And coming down again.
The Scottish six-days cycle trials
When Edinburgh drives for miles and miles
In rainbow-painted, suped-up wrecks
To watch their fellows break their necks.

It looks like Brighton or Southend
The ton-up boys are everywhere.
Their followers over backwards bend
To ape the wonderful clothes they wear,
The multi-coloured anoraks,
And quite extraordinary hats,
Petroleum Company boiler suits
And socks turned down over welly boots.

While down at the Inn a terrible din,
Unseasonable crowd,
An excuse for a drink, and to say what they think,
They voice their opinions loud
On revs and gearboxes and carbs
For many hours afterwards,
Then one last beer and stow their gear
For they'll take the day off again next year.

SEA

With dreamy opalescence you explore
and hold the glossy pebbles in a hand
lace-cuffed and intimate, or
brush with a silken fingertip the sand
on which I play. Sand ribbed and furrowed,
coiled in casts of crusted worms,
dimpled where razor-fish have burrowed
down into safety, till the tide returns
to claim the puddles and abandoned life,
the stranded butter fish, and crabs, beneath the weed
which shelters them, for opportunity is rife
for shoreline birds to search and catch and feed.
The oyster-catchers' pied and orange flight
and probing scarlet bills, the gulls who crack
open mussels on the rocks, sandpipers who alight
to search for tiny shrimps among the wrack.
Keen as bare-legged herons in the bright
shallows, among the floating, tangled weed
we stalk the shoals of sand-eels, which take fright
with synchronised, quicksilver, darting speed.
At lowest ebb, the undulating kelp
that looks like highly-polished leather gloves,
waves in the water, signalling for help
neglected by the element it loves
And then we join the predators, with pails,
to hunt for winkles, coated with a dusky sheen
and clustered on the stones. These grazing snails
we gather, for a penny each they mean
to us, who nickname them "black gold"
and search as keenly ever as wader's bill,
even when feet and fingers, numb with cold,
can scarcely scoop them up, our buckets fill.

I'm thinking of the islands in the bay
where sometimes with my brothers I explore
the tidal pools' transparent pink array
of crusted coral and anemones, or
scramble on the rocks where orange wrack
which crowns the boulders, looks like ginger hair.
When barnacles feel the water coming back,
and wave their tiny fingers in the air,
a slushing, sighing, gurgling sucking sound
accompanies the rushing tidal flow,
and everywhere above, on higher ground,
kaleidoscopic summer flowers grow.
The mustard-coloured lichen in the splashzone,
clumps of pink-headed, nodding thrifts,
grass of Parnassus sheltered from the crash
of breakers in protected clefts and rifts.
Bluebells so thick we cannot walk with care,
0 0 0 • 0 pnmroses, campwn, creepmg JUmper,
and overhead the sea birds everywhere
wheeling and crying in a frenetic stir.
Over the back, among the seaward cliffs
each bird defends a fraction of a ledge
for nesting on. With squabbles squawks and tiffs
each tries to push the other off the edge.
So many birds in constant carnival,
the guillemots in summer black and white,
the kittiwakes and cormorants, the gulls
and razorbills in alternating flight,
and down below the cliffs, the water too
is thick with birds, who swim and skim and dive
for fish, and sometimes we can see a few
porpoises jump for joy that they're alive.

Beyond these islands where the sea birds nest,
a long and oily swell, on summer night,
reflects the dying embers in the west
in technicolour shades of fractured light.
Taffeta shot with all the gemstone hues,
rose-quartz and topaz change with amethyst,
and opal with sapphire and midnight blues,
while through it is woven gold and metallic schist.
Because it is our favourite fishing ground
we row out in our little wooden boat
into the open water of the sound
to trail our lines, as dreamily we float
on all this liquid colour, till a bite
distracts and animates, and hauling line
we see the green and silver fish, and fight
it's streaking energy which flashes and churns the brine.
Out of the sunset, just to spoil our sport,
riding formation, dorsals sharp and black,
contending with us for the fish we've caught,
the giant kingfish come in to attack.
They hunt in packs, and having found our shoal
they dive and thrash beneath our little boat.
Nearly as long as it, they turn and roll,
showing their piggy eyes and pallid throats.
We head for home and leave the catch to them,
scared of their size and strength, these mini-sharks.
and now the shifting colour of the gem
has turned to malachite, for it is getting dark.
But twilight brings the herring fry ashore,
so floating in a hushing velvet glow,
encircling with phosphorescent oar
we net the slippery harvest from below.

The shining days, which memory recalls,
but many another mood you can display
of sloppy indolence, the creamy train
with which you wear your satiny silver grey.
Or when you're flirting with a north-west breeze
and in a pretty blue and white you dance,
with lots of little tripping steps, to tease
the patient beach awaiting your advance.
And when you sulk and glower with thunderous frown
we soon forget our summer in the sun,
and pull ashore the boats and batten down
knowing that when your tantrums have begun
they're likely to go on for many days.
And while you rage and scream and tear your hair
and throw yourself about in wilful craze
we watch with admiration for your flair.
The fisher-women call you slut, you lure
their men and steal their hearts away.
You are not really evil I am sure
but childishly capricious in your play.
From algae-covered rocks that shine and stream
with furious flying spray, I watch
successive mighty mountains break and cream,
topple and fall with pounding roar, to catch
at the shingle, sucking it back with crack
and crunch and squelch and tumble in greedy undertow,
then drawing yourself up for new attack
in lurid green and cobalt, grey and black,
upon the cringing helpless shore below.

It's Coronation day and I am eight,
we set out in the morning in the sun,
to go to Church, to pray and celebrate
before the evening's revelry and fun.
But setting out for home an evil hour
besets us as we leave the harbour, for
a squall so sudden, of such vicious power,
makes turning back "as dangerous as go o'er".
We have to keep our head into the wind
because the heavy sea is short and steep,
and try to leave the weather-shore behind
by heading out into the threatening deep.
Down in the trough the towering rollers seem
unclimbable. We wallow in the trench,
so slowly stagger up the hideous green
ascent, whose curling top prepares to drench
us all. Then hover there in space,
in awful view of all the monsters stacked
before us, and with sheets of water in the face,
till down we plunge with stomach-lurching smack.
Over and over, up and down, the further out we go,
and terror gets acquainted with my mind.
It all goes on and on, time goes so slow
until the shelter of the further shore we find.
And still it isn't over.

For a while by following the coastline, in the lea,
we gain a less ferocious half-a-mile,
but have to cross it in a following sea.
It doesn't seem so bad this suck and roll,
though actually it is, courage revives,
competing with the horror in my soul.
It seems that after all we may survive.

How can I ever trust you any more?
Your lovely smile can take my breath away,
but now I pace, distractedly, before
an exhibition of your violent temper, pray
that my fisherman is safe and will return
and all the other fishermen who keep
vigil with you, their daily bread to earn
upon the troubled waters of your sleep.

THE WHALE

A cold snap in November with
an icy sky and sea of slate,
scuffed and striated by the gusting wind.
The ground was iron-bound, stone cold,
no icicles or hoar,
grasses and leaves freeze-dried
to crisp fragility,
cracking and shattering under attack
from the east.

He came in on the surface, on the slack,
sleek and black, his bow-wave streaming out
in creamy whey.
From time to time he blew,
off-centre, about ten o'clock,
and the wind caught the jet
and fanned it into spray.

Circling, slowly, seeming to search each bay,
taking his time,
then as the tide turned, making up his mind
and heading for the shore.

He beached himself, deliberately it seemed,
just as the tide was starting to withdraw,
as close as he could get to the burial ground.
A whole community lies here,
huddled around an ancient yew, and dry-stone sanctuary,
the fallow out-crop butting on the sea
to form a sheltered bay.

He lay in shallow water, huge, immovable,
unmoving, till he breathed
at long intervals,
each rasping snort of air
hanging there heavily rancid, for
the wind had dropped and day begun to fade.
A winter sunset seemed to gild
the water with a platinum sheen.
The great tail lifted languidly
and molten liquid streamed from it's silhouette
The sun sank.
The tide seeped.
Suddenly his buoyancy was gone
so that he rolled his, blow-hole under
and began to drown.

Whatever motivation brought him here
with calm deliberation, fear of death
dissolved in frenzied panic
as he fought to right himself
His tail, so elegant before,
battled the golden water to a froth,
and cracked the silent twilight like a shot;
his lower jaw searched franticly
for purchase on the seabed, tried
and tried, subsided;
he was dead.

During the night the wind went round
to fill the tide.
the next ebb left him high and dry, aground

News travelled and the morning brought
a muffled audience to stare
and speculate, kids scrambled high
above their parent's heads,
poking the glaucous eye, feeling
the skin, now dull and dry, peeling
and rubbery like nioprine,
and scarred from a life of skirmishes.

The jaw was slack, each tooth could fill a hand,
the tongue hung, swollen from a crimson throat
and spermaceti leaked onto the sand
solidifying into stalagmites of lard,
Carrara-white, the purest solid lubricant there is,
and used by N.A.S.A. in pursuit of space.
Dogs raced the forty seven feet from head to tail
but didn't like the smell,

nor did the seabirds scavenge from this carrion
whose salvage rights, apparently, were Royal property.
What would have been a blessing, heaven sent,
a winter's meat and heating-oil,
roof-rafters, perfume, jewellery,
was causing an environmental incident.

Vets from the College came and diagnosed.
They took their samples with a power-saw.
Director ofEnvironmental Health [el san]
proposed a burial, a digger clawed the frozen ground,
a few feet found the water-table, so
this plan aborted as unsuitable.
The Coastguard tied an anchor to it's tail
with heavy chain and orange plastic buoy
to stop it floating on the high spring tides
and threaten navigation.
Police cars, two of them, all day,
presumably they came to see fair play
and guard the rotting carcass for the Nation.

Eventually the Navy sent a tug,
but not until the neap tide when
the cadaver was fast.
All the spectators gathered round the bay,
the Fish farm boys and local fishermen
puttered about in little boats
to ferry ropes;
the tail was tied;
until at last, with much palaver,
engines roaring as it tried to stay,
this huge embarrassment was towed away.

DEEPWATER

Her life was stuck on auto while it tumbled her along,
usually on her own,
a good wife to the house.
But now the kids are gone
it flows more slowly, long stretches passionless
where silt settles.

Returning from the sea
he is full of the tide and it's contesting power,
hovering at her shoulder in case she gets it wrong
or leaves the oven on.
Salt talk in the river-mouth,
fresh water choking back, or surging
strong in spate.

They need a delta or a hinterland,
somewhere to renegotiate the rules of war,
or peace, or home,
somewhere to cultivate,
to grow mangroves.

FISHERS

They sit on stools along the bar, in need of warmth
not only fire in the cockles and the coals, but in he heat

of many moments while they tell their fishers tales
and stoke each others embers, stroke for stroke.

Eventually they feel sufficiently restored to venture forth
to homes, warmed-over meals and tepid beds.

And after restless nights of noisy wind, with breakers
banging heads off cliffs, a morning wakens to a cool

and placid bay, the colour drained away and washedout
sky that seeps into a smudged horizon, faded

islands trailing mist, a long swell like the shallow
breathing of a pale and sleeping breast, and on a rock

against the sky, the dark cross of a cormorant which stands
with wings extended, hanging itself out to dry.

HEADROOM

I walk the bay in search of you, and see
your face reflected in the storm, in torn
tormented clouds and broken sea,
the headland hiding in the driven spray.
This tattered wrack, the undertow,
there's salt in all your wounds.

I'll try to find a windbreak or an overhang
and get myself some shelter in it's lea.
The rain is horizontal and my clothes are thin
my shoes are worn, the soles are letting in,
and till this squall is over I must keep
my head above the winter weather, but
I'll put you on the windward side and if
you even try to keep me dry,
I'll let you in.

HIGH FLYER

The stallion bucks and prances, fresh
as the always-greener grass.
The trainer stands his ground.
How long, exactly, is a halter rope,
and which the end that ties the other down?
I've always thought that it was me
who held the kite-string, watched it swoop
and fly against the wind, and checked it's stagger,
reeled in when the wind began to die.
I've never dared to fly,
to trust the rope to hold me in the air.
Up there I would be looking down
to check the knots, notice the wear and tear,
or try to read the breaking strain, the terms of warranty.
The rope is straining, holding me in place;
the kite is out of sight, and so intent on play
it doesn't know
that I could just let go and walk away.

CASTING OFF

He struggled like a fish, enjoying it
and played me for an angler till I had
to let him go. So now the line lies limp
and tangled, dredging the bottom, snagged
in reeds and sedges at the river's edge.
There must be something else to do with
all this water, shadowed amber, honey-coloured
power, dragging the trailing branches of an
anchored tree, but I am free, and I could
weave a boat, and float, or learn to swim,
and it could carry me to places I have never
been before, or it could overturn and drown me.

FOOTLOOSE

The picture of the palm trees and the blue, blue sea,
the strip of golden sand, turned out to be a mud bank
full of mangrove roots and fiddler crabs, a bar between
the water and the land. The meadow-seeming green
molinea grass is growing from the tussock-islands
floating on the bog; the log-bridge rolls, familiar
stepping-stones are washed away. It's hard to know
which way the tide is flowing, where it's safe to stand
and as the world grows dark, my lantern gutters
in an unaccustomed gust and throws my shadow
on the shifting sands. I clutch a clump of cloud berries
and hope that they will hold me, briefly, in their hands.

TO INFIDELITY

How many waifs are trailing in your wake?
Floundering flotsam floating in the trough
Of oily-bubbled back-wash, for the sake
Of your momentum though the daring, rough
And broken seas which you must always breast
With proudly pitching prow and heaving hull.
Ever a new assault upon the crest
Another wallow in the following lull.
Or unexpectant mothers cast-away
On islands of uncertain sanity
So that the other vessels in the bay
Can curtsey to your independent vanity.

Where will they go, these children of the sea?
Riding the currents, drifting with the tide,
Among the empty bottles, tangling weed, and freeRanging
rubbish from the harbour-side.
One of these days they may catch up with you
And foul your screw.

IDENTITY

To be and who to be? this question must
Be answered a copy of my life,
For all the roles I play in others trust
As daughter, sister, other, friend and wife.
I seemed to be my father's favourite son
And learned my brothers' counterfeit to be
Until I met a girl could become
Boyhood exchanged for femininity.
And so a borrowed woman I became
And acted in another masquerade
Till you who give, yet no dependence claim
All my disguise unnecessary made
By asking nothing but integrity
You and your love have taught me to be me.

The fish are gone tonight,
reincarnated stars,
to hunt the void
and haunt the waning moon.
The darkened water waits,

remembering

the creak of oars,

and spars,

and tackle,

staking creation's fortune

on the lure

of a tide.

LOST AT SEA

It's getting dark at sea, and cold.
The colours of the buried sun conveyed
On all the slow-moving shoulders,
Gun-metal shoulders, smeared with marmalade.

The shifting shapes are fishing-boats
That shadow the seamless swell, their riding-lights
Lifted, then swallowed out of sight,
Sprinkled, like Gemini, across the starless night.

Drifters, free of the wind and tide,
Their echo-sounders warn them of the reefs
And shoals, and Decca is their guide,
They have no need of stars, or of beliefs.

By now the sea is empty, not a sign
Of landfall on the scanner, or fish-blips on display,
No sound but the water slapping the hollow hulls,
Or of itinerant winds fretting the tensile stays.

The fish are gone tonight, reincarnated stars,
To hunt the void, haunt the dishonoured moon.
The darkened water waits, remembering the creek of oars and spars
And tackle, stalking creation's fortune on the turn of a tide.

ACCEPTANCE

If ever you feel that your soul has died
And the colour's washed out of your world,
When your eyes are like windows with no-one inside
In the shroud of your misery furled,
Don't put up the shutters and bury your dead
In a lonely and secretive grave,
Or challenge the phantoms that rise in their stead,
In a desperate attempt to be brave.
For a battle with truth is a battle lost
Where the victory lies with the slain
And the pride of the fight is the cause of the cost
For it poisons whatever you gain.
Make your peace with the shadows that darken your sight
For the deeper the shadows the stronger the light.

TIME AND AGAIN

Trains and buses come and go
on bright expectant Friday nights
and Sunday afternoons, while through the week
the silver birches weep their golden leaves, and day by day the sun's
appearances are lower and less long
along the ridge, till like a bouncing ball
it loses energy and doesn't rise at all.

Mergansers come in winter, black and white
and rusty- tufted ducks, who weather cold
grey seas till breeding time; and helliborus
heralds spring in snowbound drifts ofLenten
roses; ground is turned for sowing and the
seeds sift through my fingers with the past.

They say the present is like water cupped
in hands unclasped, ungrasped. I hold my peace.

TRUTH OR DARE

Peel me an onion, skin by skin
or count a tree-trunk's incremental rings
to the heartwood.
Start to unpack a baboushka doll
that's hiding womb in womb.
Unmask, unpick, unravel,
wool on a fence,
a swallow's nest with winter coming on.

Paint me a picture of the east,
a stylite's pillar in the wilderness
a lama's hermitage.
What do they hope to see?
Are angels migratory? Whispering by
to dip a wingtip in the sand
or blow some halo bubbles
and balloon away

Cry me an ocean wide and deep
or launch a dreamboat into the tide
when the moon is new.
A spider's raft that shoots the green,
a parachute to colonise the wind.
·The shaken reed can carry a tune
and float it over the air
to see if it echoes there

COLOURING-IN

I stuck some laurels in ajar of glycerine
and turned them chocolate brown and lustreless
to gather all the dust of uselessness
for years.

I don't find laurels comforting to settle on.
They smell too much of afternoon, long-shadowed
pedestals, November wreaths. I need
a greener spring, a catapult to kick me into life,
a bump-start, second-fling, a crack at Paradise.
But call them "bay", discover them in glossy racing green
and taste the aromatic heat of southern hills
where golden husks of artichokes, and silver
thistles, cling to a rocky promontory high
above the sea. And see the colours I could settle for,
for now.

TIME

Like marrum-grass
That clutches at the dunes of running sand
The moments pass
Adrift between the ocean and the land,
Where footprints fade
As one by one they fill and turn aside
Impressions made
By wanderers along the approaching tide

In aimlessness
Uncharted tracks traverse the littoral
Directionless
At first, but from a distance, over all,
They seem to be
Converging like the fibres of a web.
Infinity
Spins all dimensions into a single thread.

EILIDH AND ANIMUS

Young Eilidh was a bonny girl, she knew that she was bright,
She meant to work for her exams, say what her boyfriend might.
He didn't seem to care about the Highers drawing near,
They'd fallen out about it, and he'd left her close to tears
And gone off to a party, with another girl in tow
Behind him on the motorbike, because she wouldn't go.
She wandered home in misery and didn't even see
The glory of the spring-time in the lonely rowan tree.
She sat beneath it thinking of the way he'd let her go,
And rowan blossom drifted all around her like the snow.
It fell upon her trendy clothes, her jeans and clompy shoes
While feelings and ambition battled over what to do.
She emptied out her piece-box, spreading crumbs for birds to eat,
And didn't notice that there was a raven at her feet.

She heard the drowsy insect-hum, the curlew's mournful cry,
She felt as if she had a speck of stardust in her eye,
She rubbed it, absentmindedly, and then she saw a lad
Was standing right in front of her, magnificently clad
In every line and gesture, from the halo of his hair
Through supple limbs and golden skin to feet as light as air.
He wore the softest leather with an adder's skin for belt,
And round his slender shoulders was a mountain-lion's pelt.
His face was young, his tawny locks cascaded round his head,
He offered her a slim, brown hand, "Come dance with me" he said.
She looked within his golden eyes, his eyes of laughing fire,
All other feelings melted in a blast of strange desire, She touched his
hand, and suddenly her arms and feet were bare,
She wore a dress of tattered green, with blossom in her hair.
For seven days and seven nights he held her in his gaze,
And all the time his amber eyes were merrily ablaze.
Her body swayed exhaustedly on feet which ached and bled,
And everywhere she followed him, and everywhere he led

They crossed the shrinking snow-fields of the highest mountain
range, The Caledonian forest, prehistoric, dark, and strange.
They passed the fairy islands in the depths of Loch Maree
And came, by bogs and moorland, to the lonely northern sea.
Across the stormy waters, in a kind of magic flight
They danced, and danced, beneath Aurora's pale and ghostly light,
In megalithic circles of a people long since fled,
And tombs of ancient heroes from a culture of the dead.
On to a land of ice and fire, "Here ruled a maiden queen
As valiant a Valkyrie as any that was seen
In old Valhalla, Odin's court, in lovely Freya's reign
When maidens joined in combat for the bravest of the slain.
Brunhild, the queen, was beautiful and proud as she was brave,
And Sigurd, who had killed a dragon in its treasure cave,
Awoke her love, but left her for a princess far away,
Whose brother, Gunner, wanted Brunhild's kingdom in his sway.
She ringed herself with magic fire that mortal could not cross,
She would not let another man console her for her loss,
But Sigurd, on his magic horse and wearing Gunner's guise,
Breached her defence, and claimed her hand for Gunner, with his lies.
Unhappy Brunhild, when she found that she had been betrayed
By Sigurd, killed him and herself' He made the pictures fade
And they were dancing on the shore, in lava-coloured snow, But in
his smiling eyes there was a bright volcanic glow.

He led her to the silky-haunted skerries in the west,
And there they found a weary swan with tears upon her breast.
"I'm weeping for my brothers three, lost on the ocean wind,
We were enchanted long, ago and left our home behind."
"Fingula,do not weep", he said, "for in a little while
Your brothers will return, and you must go to Glory Isle
To seek the holy man, who will, with silver chains, release
You and your brothers from your woe, and give eternal peace."
Across the sea they danced away, the breakers at their feet,
And heard the eerie singing of the maidens of the deep
Who lure the lonesome fishermen onto the fatal shore
OfErin's green and lovely isle. "Here lived in days of yore,
When Connochar was Ulster's king, a girl whose beauty rare
Outshone the dewy morn of May, and all its flowers fair.
Concealed she was from eyes of men for fear she would inflame
Their bloody passions--which she did, for Dierdre was her name.
When Connochar discovered her and took her for his own,
She saw and loved another man and wanted him alone,
Naois, son ofUisnech, the hero ofhis day,
She followed him and won his heart, and with him ran away
Across the sea to Scotland where they lived a happy year
Till Connochar sent messengers to him, who had no fear,
Persuading him to bring his Dierdre back across the sea,
With words of friendly kinship, to a great festivity.
Though Dierdre was afraid, and did not want to leave her home
Of gentle woods and water, they set off across the foam
To Ulster, where they were beset by cruel treachery,
For Connochar used cunning and his Druid's wizardry.

In spite of all the hero's strength and courage in the fray
The King made sure with magic that they could not get away.
A wood he threw in front of them, and then an icy sea
With frozen waves of poisoned steel that wounded mortally.
Naois, bearing Dierdre, struggled on until he died.
The magic water disappeared, and left her at his side.
She bade her enemy to dig a double grave
So she could die beside the love she couldn't save."
The tale was done, the moon was full, they danced away the night,
And all the time his fiery eyes were flashing with delight.
"Now Eilidh, you have seen the lore from which your soul is bred,
You have to choose to be yourself, or one of them", he said.

He stopped beside a little hill she'd never seen before,
She saw a subterranean light behind a secret door,
He held her very close to him and asked her for a kiss,
A pledge of immortality, a sign that she was his.
She looked away a moment, but a moment was too long,
For in that moment he, the hill, and everything was gone.
The sun was down, a clammy mist was swirling all around,
She found that she was lying on the cold and stony ground.
Her shoes were scuffed and tatty, and the grass had stained her jeans
In secret accusation for the wearing of the green.
Her heart was breaking in her breast, her body wracked with pain,
She knew with bitter certainty her love had been in vain.
The raven croaked a harsh farewell from somewhere in the air,
And ever afterwards she wore the blossom in her hair.

A MIDWINTER'S NIGHTMARE

She walks alone, her solitude is freely chosen,
Unfettered, unencumbered, by the claims of children,
Or the tyranny of men.
She walks in guarded woods, in secret, dark, domains
She is her own protection from the simple pains
Of living, loving, whether good or ill,
Stalking her destiny with single-minded will.

Her destiny is underfoot and leads her on
Into the winter forest. All green is gone
And naked, twisted, trees, by moonlight fed
With cold, discerning, clarity, entangle overhead.
She doesn't look about. She doesn't want to be
Dominated by this pale, aweful beauty,
But sees among the shadows on the ground
Its mirror-image, doubled, turned around
In negative; the paradox, the feeling strong in her
That's given her the name of Domina.

She doesn't doubt her purpose, or reject her fears
But hurries on, till out of silence there appears
A motley company of Christian rag-and-bone
Pressing and clamouring round Auberon's throne.
"Aquarius, aquarius", she hears his people bleat,
He disregards the manuscripts they scatter at his feet
And hers, she notices, is lying there unread.
"I am the King of Fairyland now that their God is dead."

ALL HALLOWS EVE

In pointy hats and scary masks they run and shriek and laugh
and try to spook each other in the dark, the way we used to do.

Where are our childhood ghosts? the postie's squeaky bike,
the creaking hinge of southbound geese, the hiss

of Tilly lamps at twilight, with the flutter, singe of moths;
the smell of heather-fire always brought us hot-foot to the flame

in fascination for its power, or the scents that ambush us
from long unopened drawers, and dressing-table jars.

We wait for wintertime to wreathe each other's wraiths,
we walk a skin of ice and call to one another in the night

our echoes lingering like roses in November.

CHILDHOOD

Over the rainbow, under the moon
The twilit shadows play,
And Monday morning comes too soon
To chase them all away

Into the forest's daydream world,
The secret, haunted wood,
Where all the stories ever told
Are clearly understood.

There's magic in the deepest pool
Where faint reflections pass
Like memories of beautiful
Encounters, in a glass.

His music is the echoing strains
Of sea's tremendous roar
Feeling its rhythm in his veins
And shouting on the shore

Truth is the freedom of the hills
The bleeding sky below,
The shooting star that never kills
But falls in the burning snow

And peace is a sunny Saturday
Secure and unafraid,
With all eternity to play,
For such is heaven made.

FOR ROSS

Child of the world, just passing through.
Migrating redwings, who strip bare the berry-trees
Then leave, like you,
Taking the colour too.

Child of a child without a home,
Leaves drift before an easterly gale
In all directions blown,
The way you roam.

Child of the summer, summer's fled
With you. Don't wander in the cold.
You need to find a place instead
To lay your downy head.

Child for all seasons, settle in
At last, unpack your misty smile.
When wild geese cry to you in spring
Don't wander off again.

RATIONALE

Art is the language of the soul, conferred
By symbol, Holy Grail, the cup of grace,
In unity of music, picture, word,
And universal over time and space,
Transcending history and geography,
Culture, religion, and philosophy.

The lonely sufferer whose crown of thorns
Strangles his thoughts, entangles all his mind,
Who cannot cope with intellectual norms
In our society, so sick and so unkind,
Still has a heart to feel, and eyes to see,
And ears to listen to the muses symphony.

So teach him how to listen with his soul,
Communicate through eyes and ears and skin,
Address him through the medium that the whole
Of humankind has lodged it's spirit in.
Then surely in the comfort he will feel,
The alienation of his mind will heal.

PORTRAITS

for Kristine

A fluttering bird
Trailing a broken wing
To take you in.

Bravado bristling with beard,
The best testosterone can show
That doesn't really grow.

Peeping from the "froggan green",
Fugitive all the while
A Mona Lisa smile.

Preserve appearances, the word
Pedantic, accepting no revision,
Averting chaos with grammatical precision.

A cocky dog
Wagging a tail or two
But childhood breaking through.

Earth, stoic earth
Defending truth and love
And the pain thereof.

The eyes,
The eyes are all the same,
Seeking, asking, wondering if they dare
And if you care.

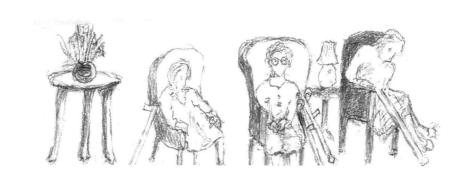

JUST VISITING

Their legs stick out like a row of stalks
in shrivelled tights and slip-resistant shoes.
and some have walking sticks, laid parallel,
with plastic tips.
Their bird-like hands, unable to keep still,
which pluck at skirts and cardigans,
are empty---idle they would once have said.
There isn't anything to do.
Their bodies sit, each in her special chair,
their minds are who knows where.

All female, they have lingered on,
they had to see their husbands through.
We do take men, we had a man quite recently'
but no-one can remember where he's gone.

This is a pleasant room, well furnished, flowers,
a bright and friendly fire. The flames are false
and warmth is coming from elsewhere,
like conversation skilfully combined
to patter over inconvenient absences
of mind and memory.

A chat-show host, incongruously,
leers from a corner unobserved.
The staff are kind, well-trained,
a culture of normality maintained
and dignity preserved.

WINTERTIME

Umber and ochre the winter grass and amber the western sky,
Purple/maroon is the scrubby birch where the ground is stony and dry,
The rest is wet and grey and sheer with the cloud hanging down to its
knee,
And the morbid bog goes loitering down to the edge of the lonely sea.
And Oh how lovely it all can be when the sun consents to shine
With a sulky temperamental charm even in wintertime,
When mosses grow and lichen, on the trunk of the leafless tree Whose
architecture is all revealed in its elegant dignity.

Everything's wet on the windward side, it rains in parallel bars,
It's barely light at half-past nine for half-a-dozen hours.
The waves that thunder upon the shore are green and menacing,
And limpid daylight mercilessly bleaches everything,
The heavy hills, the soggy glens, the saturated sky,
Dozens of little burns in unexpected hue and cry.
Water is winter's element, immersing everything,
It won't go on for very long, the snow comes in the spring.

STORM DAMAGE

The stately stands of planted pines, that tall
And straight, for a hundred years have grown,
Before the hurricane begin to fall
In serried swathes, taking each other down.
Stiff, amber-brittle branches crack and break
And snap their scented fingers at the blast,
Their upturned roots enormous craters make
As timely ripped from footholds of the past.
Are these the hollow men cut down at last?

Where light from heaven can, with the breezes blow,
In place of these authoritarian trees,
An undergrowth of scruffy species grow
And populate the country as they please,
Providing shelter and protection for
Another generation's tender brood,
As pioneering birches, once before,
Were necessary nurses to great Caledon wood.

FEBRUARY

If spring should come, however late and slow,
Thickening stems and buds with sticky glue
And crocuses appear amid the snow, >"'
Intrepid flowers, purple and gold and blue.
If birds should bravely sing from frosty tree
And earth should smell of mossy, leafy mould,
And yellow gorses scramble up the scree
Where icicles retain their steely hold,
Then hope endures and brings a joyful thrill,
Anticipation has the beat of time
Or wings, to soar above the winter chill
Into the future of a warmer clime,
And all the hoary days that intervene
Cannot obliterate the promised green.

FOR ELIZABETH

Rose-petal rain
With overpowering sense of all-in-vain,
Which tinges brown
The pastle tints of blossoms overblown,
And bows their heads
In tangled, drooping, weeping flowerbeds,
Monotonous
Dripping, arrhythmic, unharmonious.

After the rain
The bravest lift their faces up again,
Springing away
From heavy fetters, sorrow and decay.
Diluted sun
Ghosting the scented vapours, on the run
From warmer air,
And turning tears to diamonds everywhere.

ACHILTIBUIE

Thou grey and restless shingle strand
Stretching away to vast indefinitecy,
Thou greenless, wind-inviting land,
Eternity is crying out for thee.
In shallow, undeceiving sun
Thou liest, arms open to the breeze
Which whispers of the place from whence it sprung,
The haunting secrets of the northern seas.

Beware thy slumbering sweet content,
The lull of gentle, murmuring tide,
Thy yearning for the infinite,
Thy longing to embrace the ocean wide.
For when it comes, tempestuous and bold,
Dost wake from quiet patient dream?
And rise to meet the wild and passionate hold,
Storm-rocked, thy wistful waiting to redeem?

RAPUNZEL

Under the roof, where rafters touch the sky,
a tiny turret window,
falcon-high above the garden,
opens to the sunlight, and the wind
in tree-tops opposite,
where bumble bees are busy in the lime blossom.
The casement creaks and spiders' hammocks rock.
The settlements of dust, disturbed,
begin to spiral up into
the sun, discovering
old books and broken toys,
a faded photograph, beneath the eaves.
The shadows shield a still and silent bird
unpinnioned and unpreened.
What are these jesses that she wears?
What salt restricts her flight?
The wind above the world is made for wings
but though she flutters to the windowsill
she cannot overcome her fear of heights

NARCISSUS

The rocks are damp and shady where I stand,
invisible to you, across your pool.
You face the sun, and see your image
upright, perfect, clear.
From here among the shadows, where I lurk,
the picture is inverted, broken,
tangled in the floating weed;
you're growing back from man to child
with second-adolescence in between,
the golden age for looking-glasses,
rosy tints and cool, night-shades.
I lift a pebble, nurse it in my hand,
to skiff across the pond, to catch your eye
and make you break your gaze;
but cannot cast my stony countenance
to crack your self-reflective glaze
for fear that if the mirror shatters
you will seem to disappear.

METAMORPHOSIS

I've eaten all my mulberries and now it's time to spin.
My thread is long, and strong and very fine;
it can be twisted into fishing line
to catch the distant sound of laughing boys,
or braided into strings for violins.
But spooled to make a speel, or yarn,
it tells of life within a silk cocoon,
where light is filtered, opalescent, spilt,
the sharpest splinters softened, textured, dulled,
and life diminishes with every spindle-turn,
with every layer of opacity that mummifies and numbs;
of calluses that form on fingertips
as feeling calcifies and blurs,
till silence strangles laughter and
some fumbled gestures, dumb with loneliness
are all that's left to grope along the dark.
The final metamorphosis is beautiful
and will be free to fly away- one day.

FIRST IMPRESSIONS OF VENICE

The feeling of surprise and disbelief
attributed to Cortez and to Keats
I felt, when with a traveller's relief,
I stepped from Venice station in the heat
and stood in stunned amazement by the Grand Canal.
Silt brown and shimmering, rolling light
confronted me and held me in the thrall
of glossy, undulating, unexpected sight-

The choppy surface of this busy thoroughfare,
with back-wash slapping at the warves and quays,
rumpled reflections and distorted glare
of faded elegance from former days.
It must have changed since Tintoretto's time
when only barges and the gaudy gondolas
rippled the highway, and the haughty prime
of all this grandeur shone in the painted glass.

We took the waterbus which plys it's way
between the monuments of crumbling grace,
the funnelled wind, catching the bow-waves' spray
to blow it through my hair and in my face.
We passed the palaces of marble fame
of pastel tinctures, rosy or cream or white,
with every one an ancient noble name
from other centuries of wealth and might,

The side canals of secret, quiet allure
with gardens on the balconies and roofs,
so that the brilliant trailing flowers ensure
familiar continuity in these aloof
and stately relics of a former pride.
Only a glimpse in passing, till we disembarked,
rolling because of Adriatic tide
which feeds the historic basin of St Mark.

St. Mark's Basilica, ornate, so much
of splendour that I never could describe,
but with Byzantine atmosphere and such
a timeless, sacred aura to imbibe.
Out in the sunny square and almost cowed
by the magnificence of all around,
we sat and eat ice-cream, and watched the crowd
with feelings awed, and verging on profound.
The weaving, ever-changing pattern swirled,
with pigeons squabbling for the proffered lures
of people, come from all around the world
to jostle in umbrella-guided tours.

Confused, we scuttled back into the gloom
of narrow streets and creeping waterways,
where treachery, intrigue, and
haunt the imagination in the maze
of stealthy alleys, and jet-watered, sleek
canals, that disappearing into tunnels dark,
breathe the miasma of a fetid creek
with oozing banks. The tourist rout is marked
to lead us through this labyrinth between
dark-windowed, sun-precluding walls,
and issuing now and then upon a scene
of brilliant sunshine, squares with market stalls,
tow-paths along the watery cul-de-sacs
that carry traffic through the city, boats
for sewage, ambulance and fire, bric-a-brac
for tourist shops, on lorries, all afloat.

We crossed by bridges, steeply stepped to let
the water-traffic underneath them pass,
through cobbled corridors, with doors inset
of curious shops that sell Murano glass.
To Shylock's bridge, now tourist restaurant
we came, but persevered with our itinery
until, delighted by the evening chant
of blackbirds, we found the Gothic Friary.
What beauty in the arched and vaulted aisle
where once in darkly-polished choir
was sung the sacred office, all the while
and even now, to prayer and holiness it does inspire.

In candle-light we found a place to eat
and dined on shellfish, thinking of our day,
of Titian, Donatello, and the feat
of Veronese on the Doge's Golden Way.
Till lightning lit, with sudden ghostly glare
this ghostly city, and the pouring rain
sucked from the sticky pavement to the air
mosquito clouds. We ran to catch our train.

BACK TO BASICS

There isn't any point in raking through
The tepid ashes of our old regrets
To heap upon our brother's head anew,
They'll all be blown away when we forget.
Exhuming skeletons to pick again
For scraps to cast into another's eye
Disturbs their rest and resurrects the pain
Of all the crimes for which they had to die.
To close the books unbalanced, waive the score,
Is heresy in the accountants' eyes,
But how can we be accountants anymore?
The pound of flesh, the bloodless compromise,
The compensation, and insurance claim,
The quality of mercy put to shame.

DRUTH

This arid desolation of my mind
Frustrated tears of mine can never drench,
This barren wilderness of wasted time
No distillation of a morning rose can quench.
The towering thunderheads I cannot reach,
Or lightning flashing in the western sky
But leave imagination on the beach
Of bleached and desiccated bones to die.

Unless in emptiness an echo sings
Out of the well of misty memories
Of Holy Isle, the resting place of kings,
Recalling Ossian's trickling melodies.
Then can J leave my weariness to soak
In all the liquid music of the fairy folk

NO PRISONERS

I met him at a wedding once
and he was well away and in full cry.
it's always hard to hear what people say
but you can catch the tone, the stridency
and you can look- -into forsaken eyes,
and see the brow receding, tilting back,
and watch the tell-tale mouth,
the way the skin around it folds.
I wrote to him and got a brief reply.
I read some of his work, but without joy.

Elaborate paper housing schemes are built
on ground still full of caves, and cave lives
echoing from the past, and full of dreams.
Elusive fears and unexplained remorse
creep into night-time streets and hide till day.
Denial doesn't make them go away.

EYES ONLY

Sad women let their hair hang down
in ragged aprons, puckered
lips drip bitter rime of lime
-stone skins for hollow hearts
to turn them into urns for ashes.
Talk about the taste of soap
but suck the hope from images
and blow them into garbage bags
that flap in draughty closes, where
their meaning's twisted in the blast.
Iconoclasts of road signs, wayside
shrines, ring out their verse and
hang it on the line. Bells toll
in dolorous tones of voice.
The clappers clap.

ORNITHOLOGISTS

I know an ornithologist, in fact I know a few
And just in case you're wondering I'll tell you what they do,
They dedicatetheir leisure-time and sacrifice their youth
To the interests of science and the service of the truth
By tracking down their subject-matter till they can complete
Their behavioural studies of all the birds they meet.

Like many other subjects it is highly specialised
And the areas for study must be closely scrutinised.
For quantitive analysis the student must be fit
To make graphs of distribution of the wagtail and the tit
While others less specific their attention can reserve
For they find the rarer species more exciting to observe.

Their discipline is hazy, their science ill-defined,
For suitable material is often hard to find,
In terms of methodology they vary quite a lot
For statistical comparisons depend on what you've got.
But we all profess our gratitude for everything they're doing,
Here's to the ornithologists, they keep the bird life going.

ADVENT

Out of the silence of all-knowing
Omnipotence eternally unheard,
Concept on creativity bestowing,
Spoke the almighty word.

Through him the universe became
In actuality - no thought or deed or thing
Can come to conciousness without a name
For definitive being.

Light to the darkness of the blind,
Unseen, though mightier than the sword,
By opening the windows of the mind
Sight is restored.

The word in man has power to bring
The silent sightless soul
Into the light of reasoning
To make it whole.

TO A SUICIDE

Give me a justification for my life.
Why am I here at all? What is my worth?
Does my existence profit one single soul on earth?
Have I the right to live?
Have you the right to die?
Forsaking in unearned oblivion your share of human strife.
You are unique, and like no other man
Has been, or is, or will be after you, and no-one can
Double for you or fill your debt to life
Yourself to give, others to love throughout your appointed span.

SONG

Song in a silent sigh,
The grain of wheat ready to fall and die.
Breath of eternal wind
Casting the chaff that captivates the mind.
Self-hood in embryo
Lies in the cold ground ready to grow.
Time for the desert flower,
Hereafter is the ever-present now.

REDEMPTION

The first time that a man was self- aware
he tried to hide himself in Paradise,
but Eden's shelter offered no repair;
his nakedness was there before his eyes.
No feathered wings to fold upon his breast,
no covering of graceful evergreen,
no anonymity among the rest
of nature's closely integrated scheme.
The spider does not mean to hurt the fly.
It has no motivation or intent,
but acts upon a set of stimuli
and eats the meal which Providence has sent.
Nor does the bee deliberately decide
its role among the communistic swarm,
co-operative needs must always guide
its actions, in a predetermined norm.
And man was once a member of the herd,
obedient to the promptings of his soul,
a brother to the animal and bird,
a partner in the universal whole.
Now with a conscious image of himself
he stood divided, separate, apart
from blissful ignorance, security itself,

and terror coiled itself around his heart.,
Turning reluctantly from infancy,
to new and intellectual extremes,
developing material efficiency,
regaining safety only in his dreams;
till, in another garden at another time,
another man, alone and terrified,
confronted consciousness and all its crime,
accepted fear, and so its power denied.
If Paradise is not forever lost,
if self-awareness can become a key,
if innocence which intellect has cost
is mirrored in creation's mystery,
then human enterprise must be a quest,
the boundaries of knowledge be its goal,
reflecting in expanding consciousness
the elements which constitute the soul.
Only through understanding can we break
the suffocating stranglehold of fear,
which masquerades as prejudice and hate
and all the "isms" which we hold so dear.
Free from his fear, enlightened man can find
his way towards the spiritual release
where all the scattered fragments of his mind
are re-united in enduring Peace.

KNOWLEDGE

The lust for knowledge captured man's desire
In Paradise when Adam ate the fruit,
Olympus, when Prometheus stole the fire,
When curiosity left Psyche destitute.
Pandora's box held hope as well as vice
And wisdom was Prometheus' other gift,
Psyche still sleeps for love, and her advice
The son of Adam came from death to lift.
By dying between two thieves, upon a tree
He wiped the slate of that first heinous theft
Of knowledge, which can both good and evil be
And which in such confusion man had left,
So that the light of everything that's true
Can shine on those who know not what they do.

KARMA

The spirit moves upon the deep,
The living waters flow,
Over the earth the heavens weep,
The winds of karma blow.

Seasons and cycles, dust to dust,
The Karmic laws preserve,
Immutable, but always just,
We get what we deserve.

Not retribution or revenge,
Consequence follows cause.
Can we expect the Lord to change
His own creative laws?

And if what providence provides
He takes away again,
Like Job, on fortune's ebbing tide,
We have no rights to claim.

We prejudice our destiny
And seal each other's fate,
With democratic equity
We punish those we hate.

But Karma isn't punitive.
Can we impute to it
The kind of justice which we give
When we in judgment sit?

Out of the deep a cry is heard
And mercy falls like rain,
Fulfilling in the living word
The Karma of our pain.

FREEDOM

Why are you crying on the ground
Nursing an ancient wound?
The grass is growing all around
The meadow flowers in bloom.
Shake off despair, and take to the air.
The haymakers approach.
Let them not find you in the snare
Of guilt and self-reproach.
Fly to the tree that sets you free
Where justice has been done.
Take wing and sing in thanksgiving
The Victory is won

EVIL

If God made everything, no matter how,
And of Himself is infinitely good,
Then evil cannot be as we allow,
But must be differently understood.
It cannot be an actuality
But has to be an absence, or a dearth
Of Goodness' positive potentiality
For love and growth and happiness on earth,
As, when a cloud obscures the morning sun
A shadow creeps upon the land below,
And all the flowers that have just begun
To open, close their eyes again and cease to grow.
So if our world's condition we deplore
We'll have to try to love each other more.

CREDO

The One who dwells within is part of us as we are part of Him,
But locked away, a prisoner in dungeons dark and dim
At depths we do not wish to know,
Guarded by Ego's whim,
Unless we dare to go below
We can't get near to Him.

But in our underworld with eyes alight,
Reflected in His eyes, as He in ours,
The warmth and peace of being there, the gentle light
Illuminates our intellectual powers.
Till Ego's tyranny and rampant will
Can gradually be tempered in the fire,
The Gaoler's vigilance relaxed and still
Allowing passage to our heart's desire.

The passage isn't easy though, the flight is steep,
And slippery and treacherous the stair,
The Gaoler often wakes again, restored by sleep
To wrathful arrogance and mean despair.
For all our armour of philosophy,
Thoughts and beliefs supposed to conquer doubt,
Religion's antidote to sophistry?
We wear 1t ups1de-down and ms1de-out.

The point of symbols is that they unfold
A magic carpet straight to the underworld.

MARTHA

The conscientious woman must be up before the sun
On washing days and market days. There's ironing to be done
And floors to sweep and rugs to beat and cleaning out the grate
And a host of preparations so the dinner won't be late.

But why the hurry and the fuss?
Who cares about a little dust?
Dust will be with you always like the poor.
An unironed collar gives no pain
Will soon be in the wash again
Don't let such details make you insecure.

As for the culinary feats
The special breads and kosher meats
The finger-bowls and rigmaroles
Required by Jewish protocols-
Come and sit down and rest your feet.
It doesn't matter what we eat.
You need some time to be yourself
So leave the mending on the shelf,
To think and wonder, maybe dream,
And do the house work in between.

REQUIEM

A single wreath upon the alter- step,
A congregation young and overwrought,
Grief and confusion that they can't forget,
Into Saint Agnes sanctuary had brought.
Not smartly, nor conventionally dressed,
No compromise formality to please,
As close in mind as bodily compressed,
Where tragedy had brought them to their knees.
The unity and power of that prayer,
Drawn from intense emotions unrepressed,
And tangible as static in the air,
Could not have failed in winning its request
From him in whom all anguish is redressed
And tragedy transformed to something blessed.

A QUIP

You cannot prove that God is there,
Thomas Aquinas can you hear?
He wouldn't be omnipotent
If reason could be paramount,
You have to just believe in him
Or not, according to your whim.
And if you do, it follows still
That nothing is impossible
For Him. Whatever way He acts
Argument cannot alter facts.

PERSONA

The simple soul gets out of bed. What should he wear today?
Society can offer him a host of roles to play.
Next to his skin, (of black or white) where attitudes are keen
He must put on his underwear, the orange or the green?
Then comes the shirt and collar, is it white or is it blue?
Depending on his choice he'll have a different point of view,
For blue can make him truculent with rights to struggle for
While white entitles him to be a bit superior.
And what about his outer wear-- a business suit perhaps?
Or tweed plus-fours and stockings for an outing with the chaps
Some heavy gear, or bushy beard and hairy tartan shirt
To camoflage the fact that he's afraid of being hurt,
Some macho army-surplus for a swagger with the boys,
Or something cool for pulling birds, by making lots of noise.
And next he'll have to choose a tie, (or wear an open neck)
To signify an empathy with others in his set,
Old-boys or regimental for an understated dash,
While unconventionality is avant-guard or flash.
Now to decide about his hair and how to have it cut,
A vital contribution to his total image, but
A right-wing cut is very short, no compromise to leave
While shoulder-length reveals the heart he wears upon his sleeve.
With dozens of accessories in which he could be seen
Like football scarves, or golfer's caps, or wellingtons of green,
A red rose in his buttonhole, a military moustache,
A rolex or a pair of shades, and aftershave awash.
A simple soul no longer, in the mirror he can see
The complicated person that he thinks he wants to be.

Society will deal with him according to his role.
Whether he has a steady job, or if he's on the dole,
He has to be included in a statistition's scheme,
Which kind of coffee does he buy, which size of salad-cream?
And every single detail of the way he lives his life
Along with information on his children and his wife,
All go to make a profile, a computerised ideal,
Politicized and classified, which tells him how to feel
Which party he should vote for, and which newspaper to read
For he has been identitfied and issued with his creed.
Our friend is getting restless in this closely woven mesh,
He feels himself restricted and he wants to start afresh.
To try to buck the system or to jump across the wall
Is treated with suspition and as pride before a fall.
He wants to be a liberal and keep an open mind,
And hopes through education some equality to find,
But people in "establishment" are always criticised,
And teachers, for their pains are universally despised.
He can't impress the children if their parents don't approve
So kids who need his help the most are hardest to improve.
Here ends another chapter in the generation game,
The way that things are going it will always be the same.

He thinks perhaps in politics, the left-wing or the right
To get an insight into why the categories fight,
But all the vested interests he sees on every side
Make compromise impossible for common sense to guide.
It seems to be a power-struggle for a very few
Who think they have the right to choose what others ought to do.
Our simple soul has done his best and only been confused,
He thinks he'll just go back to bed, he hasn't been amused.

TO THE OUT GOING PRESIDENT OF THE U.S. OF A.

Georgy Porgy Broccoli Bush
Be quick before you get the push
To lay the spook of Vietnam
By dropping bombs on mad Sadaam

He spoilt your re-election plan
So get you're own back while you can
You've still got time before you quit
To try and rub his nose in it.

You're going to have to give your toys
As hand-me-downs to other boys
So while they're still your own to use
Why don't you have a game with "Cruise".

You really haven't very long
So launch your missiles, forty strong,
While they are still within your reach.
They're only few million each.

And when you've had a playful bash
By spending all the ready cash
The best is still to come -mayhap
You'll land the bill in Clinton's lap

And pay him back for beating you
By wrecking what he wants to do.
Before he's paid for what you've done
He'll come to wish he hadn't won,

For with your economic mess
And starting lots of wars, I guess
You'll really drop him in it- Hell
You'll get revenge on him as well.

YOU CAN'T MAKE AN OMELETTE

Humpty Dumpty King of the Fools,
An egotist between two stools,
Why did you set yourself so high?
You might have known you couldn't fly.

You embryonic addlebrain
Without a feather to your name,
Why did you ever leave the nest?
You might have hatched beside the rest.

Cock o' the roost you tried to be
Without his vulnerability,
Behind a brittle shell to hide
The jelly that you are inside

And found a perch from which to crow,
Your cocky consequence to show.
But even on the highest shelf,
You couldn't incubate yourself

Because you threw your weight around
You lie exposed upon the ground,
And since your precious shell you broke
Your nothing but a helpless yoke.

If showing-off you can't resist,
You childish exhibitionist,
Admit your insecurity
And don't pretend maturity.

WISDOM

The fates devise to make a wise man wise,
A woman mellow, and her lover ripe,
And so to wed them and their seeds unite
To sow and grow upon a summer's night.

For wisdom is the germ to grow unseen,
To live and graft upon the sapling green,
Developing beside the blood and bone,
Biding it's time until the youth is grown.

And so, green wood to season, pride to prune,
The sap to rise and blaze in hopeful bloom,
The bud to burst, to parch and wilt at noon,
The fruit to form, to swell and lusty ripe
For Autumn's rot and Winter's withering blight.

Till through the weathering of time,
Wind-bent, and gnarled and knotted he can stand,
And can forgive his ardent youth so brave,
Can seek, and listen, and can understand
But nothing say; then stately, hand in hand
Wisdom and age go down into the grave.

The fates devise to make a woman blind,
With many fancies in an empty head,
Her lover callow and the evening wet
Why then, perhaps, the fellow they beget
Will be a bloody know-it-all instead.

GREECE

Beloved Greece of golden light and ozone-crazy air
Heavy with insect drone and wild oregano smells,
Pine-resin, myrtle and old sun-baked stones,
The mellow tones in minor keys of sheep-carried bells.
Hot winds from the Sahara scour the mountain-scape behind
The hand-hewn terracing, olives and fruit and vines
Cliff-hanging through the mud-and-boulder-slides
Of winter's torrents, hail, and electric storms in brilliantly mad
designs

The gods have flown and left the elements to rule the roost
And wear away the remnants of their glorious reign.
They have good jobs in Academia now, as poet's inspirations,
And the leading roles on Broadway and in Dury Lane.

Plato and Aristotle emigrated West with Socrates
To be in charge of Oxbridge and affairs of state.
From Bundestag to White House their opinions can be heard
In every ponderous chamber of debate.

But Pallas Athene could not bear to leave her sunny home,
While poppies grew among the crumbling shrines she lingered there.
She did not want to see her name in lights, but watch the little skiffs
Go out at night, the old men in the coffee shops, And bright and
happy gatherings in the market-square.

CONUNDRUM

Even the greatest poets, Goethe, Keats,
Inspired to purest ecstasy of art,
The subject-matter of their finest feats
Is usually some matter of the heart.

The fairest heroines of high romance
Have to await in helpless, mute despair
Their gallant champions' valiant, swift advance
To be delivered from the dragon's lair.

The lovely Helens and the Guineveres,
The Madelines, and Ladies of the Lake
The courtly chivalry of men revere
Whenever knightly honour is at stake.

Classical painters illustrate the theme,
What quantities offemale flesh exposed,
But where romantic influence is seen
A whisp of drapery is interposed.

Some of the Goddesses of Greece and Rome
Bewilder with their gifts the artist's pen,
Though some content enough to guard the home
Others usurp the qualities of men.

Venus or Aphrodite - fair enough
Their purposes are obvious as the day,
Hester, Demeter- all domestic stuff,
There's nothing there to puzzle or dismay.

But Artemis, Apollo's moonlight twin
[Diana is the huntress' other name]
Her attributes are always masculine
Whenever hunting is a human game.

Pallas Athene, enigmatic, wise,
The arbiter of wars and strife and grief,
If seen in realistic human guise
Would be considered way outside her brief.

As for the Muses, ladies who inspire,
Supposedly, the poets' fantasy,
Surely imagination can't require
The influence of femininity?

Even impartial Justice is portrayed
As female - twist in the tail
For those who think that they have been betrayed
When men and women balance in the scale.

And Liberty- she has to be a joke.
The suffragettes are rattling their chains
Watching their sisters carrying the yoke
Which male superiority maintains.

Women, from ancient times to these
Have been adored in myth and fairy-tale
While in mortality they've had to please,
Obey, and be dependant on the male.

Is it the hope of immortality,
That Lady-loves, once lost, are always young?
Is it that sleeping Psyche is a she,
A part of man for which he will always long?

Or is the truth in paradox concealed?
Only the prisoner is truly free,
Virtue and Wisdom cannot be revealed
Except when Choice is brandishing the key?

COMPANY MANNERS

I'm only a local yokel, I haven't a PhD.
I've always belonged to the back of beyond
With innocuous idiocy.
My upbringing wasn't suburban
So I haven't the faintest idea
Of the people to con if you want to get on
In a dog-eating, rat-race career.

I'm only a local yokel,
I go to the boss's for tea
Where I gratefully take the elaborate cake
That is offered benevolently.
As I sit in my jeans and two jumpers
On the very expensive settee,
For my social mistake I must silently bake,
All the firm's central heating is free.

I'm only a local yokel,
I fancy a company car,
But I'm really so thick I don't know how to nick
And I haven't the brass to acquire.
I wouldn't say "no" to a freezer
If I knew where to get one for nil,
But I haven't the nouse for a company house
Where there's no electricity bill.

I'm only a local yokel,
There are plenty of others like me,
It's a shocking disgrace that we can't keep our place
With appropriate humility.
To superior urban behaviour
We ought to be made to agree,
And to give us a lead what we desperately need
Is a company secretary.

As long as she comes from the city
And has a contempt for the rest,
She can hold her own with a lofty tone
And will never be put to the test.
The peasants will all be subjected,
The managers kept on their toes
Well, I'm only a local yokel,
So I'd better get back to my brose.

COME THE CARNIVAL

She hadn't written since her mother died
she'd lost her balance and the rhythm of the dance.
Numb fingers, stiffened by the cold
fumbled with words and scattered t:hem harmlessly across the page.
But come the spring and come the carnival,
follow the piper, listen to the drum,
swallow the fire, juggle in the sun.
I haven't written since my mother died,
the time has come.

The ink dries up before it leaves the pen,
this paper standing sentry to its flow.
I can be still as whitewashed coal
but moving can be dangerous
and anything that moves me now must catch me on the run.
I've learned to speak with paint:
to paint with words I'll have to learn to use my legs again.

AGEING

What harm is there in standing still
And looking round me for a while
At all the lovely things that fill
My heart with joy, and make me smile?
I am not old enough for looking back
Over a lifescape's ups and downs,
The evening yet some hours lacks
For action, till the retreat shall sound,
Yet I am old enough, I'm not so keen
To hurry on, [time does it anyway]
And go without this interval between
Secret tomorrow and remembered yesterday.

I hope that I can age with all the grace
Of some old ladies' fragile dignity-
Faint, old-rose, silken-wrinkled face,
Parchement hands of veined transparency.
Fire no longer raging, but still warm,
A silver sail upon a falling tide,
The tatters made by many a former storm
All neatly patched and gently laid aside.
Perhaps an autumn garden in the sun
Awaits, where fruit can ripen on the wall
And I can doze and dream till day is done,
Only a child away from my recall.

JUST A THOUGHT

The only thing of which I feel convinced,
In spite of all the theories that abound,
Is that the truth will never be evinced
From any information I have found;
That learning brings it's own reward, though brief,
A fleeting satisfaction of the mind,
But oonscious thought, and words, and fixed belief
Are only the deceivers of the blind.
To know it all, to point the final blame
Would be a rational atrocity,
So I prefer to play a waiting game,
For happiness is curiosity.
The meaning of existence is well known
I think, that very purpose would be gone.

MOTHERHOOD

The vital welling spring
Concealed, her still and secret joy within,
Is waxing with the moon,
Locked in the hallowed, archetypal womb
Where ever child has been
Harboured, in patient happiness serene.
Till separateness
Becomes an even greater gift to bless

THE EDGE

The geese begin their southern flight,
Creaking across the sky.
The easy summer's golden light
Is hanging out to dry.
A warning crackles in the green,
By icy breezes blown,
The edge of pain that's sharp and clean
And cuts illusion down.
The fiery colours float and fall,
Fanned by October's breath.
Loveliest season of them all,
How beautiful is death.

ABOUT THE AUTHOR

Toni Maclean was brought up on a remote coastal farm in the west highlands of Scotland, without any road access or mains electricity. She had no formal education till she was nine, then she went to a convent school in Perthshire and later studied social work at Dundee university. She married a fisherman and had four sons and when they left home she took up art and writing poetry, also travelling to broaden her experience. She also continued to work with the mentally ill. She moved to Fife in 2016 and died two years later from a brain tumour. She was a devout Christian.

Printed by Amazon Italia Logistica S.r.l.
Torrazza Piemonte (TO), Italy